Raising Yourself

Raising Yourself

Making the Right Choices

COLLEGE? DRUGS?
SEX? VALUES?
PEERS?
PREGNANCY? GANGS?

THE FUTURE

Sumant Pendharkar

Hillview Books
Los Altos, California

Interior design by Pete Masterson, Æonix Publishing Group, www.aeonix.com
Cover and interior illustrations by Aldin Baroza
Edited by Richard Biegel

Publisher's Cataloging-in-Publication
(Provided by Quality Books, Inc.)

Pendharkar, Sumant S.
    Raising yourself : making the right choices / Sumant Pendharkar. -- 1st ed.
    p. cm.
    Includes index.
    SUMMARY: This compendium of comprehensive advice for teens on growing up includes sections on career options, mental and physical development and values.
    Audience: Ages 10-18.
    ISBN 0-9708131-3-9
    LCCN: 2001087800

    1. Teenagers--Conduct of life--Juvenile literature.
2. Maturation (Psychology)--Juvenile literature.
[1. Conduct of life. 2. Maturation (Psychology)]
I. Title.

BJ1661.P46 2001   158'.0835
                             QBI21-103

2 3 4 5 6 7 8   07 06 05 04

Published by:
Hillview Books
P.O. Box 3473
Los Altos, CA 94024
Phone: 650-967-4933

www.hillviewbooks.com

Printed in the United States of America

Hey Mom, Dad, you can have your job of "raising me" back anytime you like ... oh, by the way, about that allowance...

Contents

Dear Reader,

You're living in one of the richest and most advanced countries in the world. As an immigrant who has seen the world, I can personally vouch for this. Since completing my education in India a decade ago, I've traveled to countries all over the world, including Europe, Asia, and, of course, the Americas. If anything has impressed me in the years that I've worked and traveled, it is the astounding opportunities available here in the USA.

The United States leads the world in Science and Technology. Skilled workers are needed to maintain and advance this lead. The US has to rely on immigrants to staff the unfilled positions. These jobs are real opportunities, high paying and within your reach.

Whether you were born in the most distant country or in the heartland of America, you should be aiming for these jobs. With a good job, the good life can be yours.

However, to qualify for these jobs you need to start preparing for them during your teen years.

As a teen, you are in a critical phase of your life. The choices you make now will determine your future. That is what this book is all about. In the coming years, life will confront you with some of the most difficult and crucial choices you'll ever encounter. How you make these difficult and often-unpleasant choices will definitely shape your future.

This book is intended to help you see the possible effects of the decisions you make. This is very important. As you pass through the teen years, the decisions you make will decide the quality of your adult life. Of course, you can recover from bad choices, but making them in the first place can cause unnecessary, troublesome obstacles.

It really is your life, and what you decide to make out of it is your choice. Look at the big picture outlined in this book. Make your personal life choices knowing the consequences of your decisions.

And good luck in raising yourself.

— *Sumant Pendharkar*

P.S.
I would love to hear from you. Email or write to:
author@hillviewbooks.com
P.O. Box 3473
Los Altos, CA 94024

Acknowledgments

The title of this book, *Raising Yourself,* was a result of brainstorming with Kathleen Tait while eating spicy Jamaican food at Mango Café in Palo Alto, California. Thanks Kathleen.

It took two years of evenings and weekends to finish this book. However, to get to this stage, I was fortunate to get the help of family members, friends and friends of friends. Their help came in many ways — editing, reviewing the manuscript, suggestions for sections, anecdotes and experiences from their own life, encouragement and questions such as, "Aren't you done yet?" and assistance in locating resources that I needed to get the book published.

I would like to thank (in no particular order): Helena and Fernand Rasetti, Dan Poynter, Gioia De Cari, John Reidhaar-Olson, Donna Sanders, Aaron Sanders, Michele Kahn, Beth Wilson, Terry Townsend, Paige Farsad, Danni Urbatzka, Melissa Davies, Caroline Horn, Leah Talbert, Arjun, Jahnavi, Gauri and Vivek

Pendharkar, Shiven Malhotra, Joanne Giudicelli, Monica Nulkar, Vijaya and Anand Gore, Margaret and Brian Rouley, Karol and Dale Scott, Lori Hart Beninger, Matt Beninger, Richard Mezirka, Lewis Mezirka, Sunita Jayakar, Giovanni Rodriguez and David Cook.

Many thanks to Aldin Baroza for the illustrations (inside and the cover), Richard Biegel for editing the book, Diane Gibbs for proofreading it, and Pete Masterson for putting it all together.

And finally, many thanks to my wife, Medini, for letting me get away with neglecting lots of chores around the house under the pretext of finishing this book.

A Reality Check

Here are some realities.

- You are responsible for your own life.
- You need money to live. Food, housing, medicine, car, health insurance, entertainment ... all require money.
- To get money, you need to earn it.
- The amount of money you earn depends a lot on your education or the useful skills you learn.

A key component in the equation of life is *time*. It's one thing you can never get back. *Once you've lost it, it's gone forever.* Of course, you can waste your teen years using drugs, dropping out of school, getting involved in gangs, or getting pregnant. With willpower and luck you might even be able to pull yourself out. But you'll lose the most important time of your life — the teen years — which you could have used to lay a strong foundation for the future.

The end result of wasting teen years is *playing catch-up in life*. While others are enjoying their twenties and

thirties — driving expensive cars, buying homes, traveling for leisure, advancing their careers, raising a family, enjoying hobbies, giving to society — you'll probably
be in a lower-paying job, trying desperately to get the
right education and skills, and looking for a way up.

Such struggle often looks great in the movies. But
real life is a lot harder than that.

Granted, you can undo some of the worst life-chang-
ing mistakes, but this comes at a price.

Let's look at an example. Suppose you drop out of
school, work at a low-paying job, get sick of it all, and
then decide one day to go back to college. Here's the
situation you'll probably face:

- You'll have to take evening or part-time classes,
  thus prolonging your education considerably.
- You'll have costly habits that you'll have to unlearn
  (a lot harder than it sounds).
- You'll have to make significant changes to your lifestyle to save money for tuition. And you might have
  to go into debt with school loans, while your peers
  are paying off theirs.
- Once you graduate, you'll have to compete with
  graduates much younger than you are, and many
  employers prefer younger workers. (Don't kid yourself; there is definitely age bias in the workplace.)

Keep in mind that *time does not stand still*. While
you're turning your life around, changes are constantly
taking place in the job market. Jobs are regularly moved
overseas (especially manufacturing jobs). The remain-
ing jobs require a lot more skills, and technology is out-
pacing almost every other job sector. Getting a head start

could give you a crucial advantage, while falling behind could hurt you.

Life is tough. Don't make it tougher for yourself than necessary.

What Does It Cost to Live on Your Own?

Here is what it will cost you to live on your own *per month* in a metropolitan city (varies by region) in the US:

Housing (rent) . . . . (approximately) $750
Food $100
Car $200
(varies depending on outright purchase, financing, lease, etc.)
Car insurance, maintenance, gas $150
Health insurance $100
Entertainment (eating out, movies, concerts) . . . $200
Clothing, personal items $150
Cable $50
Phone $50
Utilities (water, gas, electricity, etc.) $100
Monthly Total . . . . (approximately) $1,850
   (Add extra for emergencies, furnishings, vacations, and so on.)
   Of course, you have to pay taxes, including federal,

state, local, and social security. In most cases, these taxes are deducted from your paycheck automatically. So to earn minimum living expenses *after taxes*, you'll need a total salary of at least $2,600 per month. That's over $30,000 per year.

Do you have the skills and education you need to generate a $30,000 annual income?

As an exercise, use the table below to figure out what it costs to live in your area. Individual needs vary, so figure in your personal preferences.

Category	Amount
Housing (rent)	_____
Food	_____
Car	_____
Car insurance, maintenance, gas	_____
Health insurance	_____
Entertainment	_____
(eating out, movies, concerts)	
Clothing, personal items	_____
Cable	_____
Phone	_____
Cell phone, pager	_____
Utilities (water, gas, electricity, etc.)	_____
Internet access	_____
Total	_____
Savings for emergencies	_____

Aren't you glad someone else pays for your living expenses while you are still a teen?

What You Should Do, When and Why

Phases in life

Decisions that will derail your life

Phases in life

Just as we learn to walk in phases (crawling, standing, taking that first step), we live our lives in a sequence of phases.

For most people, the phases of life could be charted as follows:

Phase I (Birth to twenties)

- Social skills
- Knowing the difference between right and wrong
- Self-discipline (taught by parents, teachers, and others)
- Personal development
- Concentrating on school, college
- Dealing with peers

- Staying out of trouble (with the law)
- Deciding on a career
- Adding skills

Phase II (Twenties to thirties)

- (optional) Graduate school
- Getting a job; staying out of debt (understanding money) and credit cards
- Employment — for someone else or start your own business
- Financial stability; learn value of money as you pay your bills and find a balance between income and expenses
- Relationships
- Parenthood

Phase III (Thirties and forties)

- Financial planning for buying a house, investing for retirement, having kids
- Coaxing your kids to go to college, ensuring career is rock-solid
- Learning new skills, volunteering

Note: I have intentionally left out the fifties and up. By that age, decisions made earlier in life start catching up, and what people do with their lives varies immensely from person to person.

Life is not "fully" predictable, and depending on many factors — decisions you make, your family background, some hidden talent, or just pure and simple *luck* — your phases in life may be very different from others'.

For example, if you are gifted in sports, music, or academics, the phases you go through may be accelerated. Bill Gates dropped out of college to found

Microsoft; Tiger Woods dropped out of college and set records by winning golf tournaments; the Williams sisters (Venus and Serena) have excelled in the tennis world. Gates, Woods, and the Williams sisters have enough money to not work another day of their lives.

But don't count on being one of these lucky people. They are extremely rare.

Decisions that will derail your life

Getting pregnant or fathering a child while still in your teens

Before you risk pregnancy with casual or irresponsible sex, think of the consequences that you're likely to face:

- *If you are female*, you've just signed 18 years of your life away to raising the child. You might have to drop out of school or college to care for the child. If the father walks out and you have no support, you'll be in a terrible financial jam. Worse, you might be dependent on the very people that you chose to ignore in the first place — your parents.

You'll have to abandon the carefree teen years and accept the responsibility.

Even if you choose to have an abortion or give up your child for adoption, you could have guilt feelings that last for a long time (or forever).

- *If you are male*, you have a

responsibility to the child and the mother. To raise the child and support the mom, you need to earn money. More than likely, you will have to drop out of school and get a job. Unless you have good job skills, you will probably earn near the minimum wage. This is a terrible hardship; think of how much income you need to have a decent standard of living, even by yourself — food, apartment, clothes, car, insurance, expenses for entertainment, and so on.

Even if you decide to walk away and ignore your obligations, the courts could hold you liable, which could drain you of your earnings even if you have a good job.

For an idea of how tough it is for a low-income family of three, look back at the worksheet on page 17. In addition to the items listed there (which don't include the additional costs of a pregnancy) add the following expenses:

- Medical insurance to cover the mom-to-be and the baby
- Prenatal care
- Delivery charges (sorry, the stork does not deliver for free)
- Hospitalization charges and medical expenses not covered by insurance
- Clothes for the baby, including diapers
- Baby food
- Medicines for the baby
- Baby-sitter
- Crib, stroller, toys for the baby

Here are some other important issues to remember.

You could marry to raise the child, but such marriages usually don't last, and it's well known that divorce is a nightmare for children. And divorce brings the added problems of alimony, child support payments, and visitation rights. Perhaps worst of all, your child will face difficult emotional problems when you try to start a new family with another person.

Please, be aware of the risk before having sex.

Ask yourself, "Am I ready to support a child?"

Dropping out of school

Hear it in Sarah's words:

At 16 I dropped out of school. I thought I knew everything and no longer needed education.

But I was totally unprepared for the harsh realities of the real world. Without a safety net from my parents, and with mounting bills, I had no choice but to work at many low-paying jobs — some paying slightly over the minimum wage. Without education and in a highly competitive job market, my options were limited.

As reality set in, my only option was to go back to school and complete my G.E.D. and eventually enroll in a college or vocational training school.

I urge you to reconsider dropping out of school. It's difficult to go back once you are out.

—Sarah, 34, San Jose, CA

What is your earning potential without an education? The US Department of Labor confirms Sarah's warning. In 1998, the median earnings of full-time workers aged 25 years and over were as follows:

	Per Hour	Per Week	Per Month
Less than a high school diploma			
	$8.42	$337.00	$1,348.00
High school graduates, no college			
	$11.98	$479.00	$1,916.00
Some college or associate degree			
	$13.95	$558.00	$2,232.00
College graduates			
	$20.53	$821.00	$3,284.00

If you completed the blank worksheet on page 18, compare your living expenses to the above incomes.

Ask yourself, "How much would I like to earn?"

Drugs

Drugs are a harsh reality of the world we live in. Mind-altering drugs are available. They lure people in because of their ability to make you feel good for a short time. Unfortunately, they usually make you feel bad (sometimes *really* bad) once the high wears off, which makes you want to have more.

You hear it from your family, your teachers, the media — "just say no," "don't do drugs." I agree. But go a step further — learn about the subject.

Before you consider taking any drugs, consider the following:

Mind-altering drugs do just that — they affect your judgment, your ability to think clearly. You might end up taking risks you ordinarily wouldn't dream of taking. You might put yourself, your friends, or your loved ones in danger.

Many now-illegal drugs were first used for medicinal purposes, but they turned out to be addictive, and had other side effects that make them dangerous. Scientists have since developed better, safer, more effective medicines. Illegal drug producers care nothing about safety or quality. For example, did you know that drain cleaners, battery acid, lye, and antifreeze are often used to make amphetamines today?

Do you know your state's penalties for drug possession? Don't kid yourself — drug possession is a crime. It is very difficult to turn your life around after an arrest. You have to rebuild the trust of your family; you may be imprisoned when you should be enjoying college. And a police record seriously hurts your chances for good jobs later in life.

How would you pay for these drugs? The "highs" associated with the most common illegal drugs last between 10 and 30 minutes. Then what? The average cost of an ounce of marijuana is $50.00, (*Source: 1996 Report, National Narcotics Intelligence Consumers Committee (NNICC), "The Supply of Illicit Drugs to the United States.") Will you need to resort to other crimes to fund your habit?

You've heard it before, and it's true — no addict ever started off saying "I want to grow up to be an addict." It sneaks up on you. Be careful. Be alert. Be informed.

Joining a gang

People usually join gangs to
- Search for belonging, and be part of a family (fellow gang members)
- Bow to peer pressure, and be perceived as cool

- Get an ego boost, find a way to raise self-esteem with macho behavior
- Seek protection from other gangs (especially in dangerous areas)

These are strong temptations, and they are seductive to many young men (and women) who live with fear, loneliness, or poverty. But whatever temporary comfort gang membership might offer, it can cause a severe setback in your life. Many people find that joining a gang is much easier than leaving it. And, of course, gang membership is the surest way to get in trouble with the law. As a member of a gang, you risk arrest and imprisonment, plus the danger of being shot (possibly fatally). **Remember, when you join a gang your family and friends can easily become victims too.**

Gun wounds are romantic only in the movies. Many former gang members live in wheelchairs because of spinal injuries, suffered in fights with rival gang members.

Even if you expect to leave a gang some day, think of the long-term consequences of joining in the first place. Are you aware that to get a good job, you must fill out a job application form, and that most applications ask if you have ever been arrested? What are your chances of getting a good job if you answer "Yes" to that question?

Whatever your life circumstances, you don't need to join a gang.

There are far better ways to achieve the things you want in life. One of the best is to get involved in volunteering, which has brought meaning and purpose to millions of people. There are hundreds of volunteer organizations to choose from, and you can find at least one that you enjoy.

Volunteering can do more than keep you out of trouble. It has lots of other benefits:

- You can achieve a sense of belonging (one reason why many teenagers join gangs).
- You can learn how to make contacts (80% of all jobs are acquired through friends and acquaintances).
- You might just find something you really like to do.
- It's good for your self-esteem.
- It's a great opportunity to build social skills, such as public speaking and teamwork.

For more information on volunteering, visit *www.servenet.org* on the Web or call 1-800-VOLUNTEER. You can search for teen-specific volunteering opportunities by zip code on the Web site.

External Factors That Influence Your Development

Your life consists of a series of events.

Yes, some events are out of your control. You can't control the weather; you can't choose your parents, your place of birth, your ethnic group, or your gender. You can't always prevent accidents, sickness, marital problems between your parents (including divorce), the death of a parent, or your family's financial problems. It's crazy to assume that you have one-hundred-per cent control over every event in your life.

Even so, many crucial events are within your control. You decide which books to read, which music to listen to, which values to embrace, which friends to keep, and how to handle problems. In fact, you will probably be confronted with real choices throughout your life. These choices not only determine how well you live; they also define what kind of person you become. As a character in a movie once said, "We are, in fact, the sum total of all the choices we have made."

Most of the important things that happen to you are at least partially under your control.

For the moment, forget the things you can't change; look at some of the things you *can* control.

- You can choose to educate yourself (high school, college, and more advanced degrees).
- You can keep mentally and physically fit.
- You can ignore temptation or peer pressure to smoke, drink, take drugs, and risk arrest.
- You can influence the direction your life takes by making smart and informed decisions and not letting anyone else make these decisions for you.

Let's see how the external factors affect your personal development.

Peers

The good

The bad

The ugly

Your opinion of yourself ... or others' opinion of you?

The good

"**A person is known by the company he keeps.**"

Heard this one before? Believe it or not, it's true.

Your friends have a very deep influence on you. Not only do you spend a lot of time with them; you're likely also to do a lot of things to win their approval.

So if you want approval from your friends (and who doesn't?), you might as well choose your friends wisely. What is the likelihood of straying from the right path if your friends have their act together? Simply by hanging out with the right crowd, you can avoid trouble automatically.

The reverse is also true. For example, if your friends smoke, you could be tempted to light up. If your friends try to pressure you into it, it could be very difficult to say no. Why? Because if you resist their pressure, they may think you are judging them, or you might feel not accepted. Choose nonsmokers as friends, and you probably won't light up at all.

One of the advantages of choosing wiser, smarter friends is that you can choose a winning life strategy without feeling left out. More importantly, there is strength in numbers. Choose the right circle of friends, and your other peers are less likely to pick on you.

Think of this: The ones who laugh at you might just end up working for you. While you're moving forward to success, they'll waste time risking their future, laying the foundation for failure and dependency on others.

Surround yourself with friends who do at least some of the following:

- use positive thinking
- have good manners
- have a good self-image
- do well in school
- do not smoke, take drugs, or drink alcohol (show some restraint or self-discipline)
- enjoy some hobby, sport, or other activity that interests you
- inspire you
- uplift you when you are feeling down
- make you feel good in their presence

Remember that most people prefer friends who are involved in common activities. If they smoke or take drugs, they'll want you to do the same.

Personally, I'm glad that I hung out with the right crowd. Now most of my friends are engineers, doctors, accountants, computer specialists, professors, and so on. Like me, they are very well placed in their careers, independent, and free to enjoy life to the fullest.

You can be too.

The bad

You are bound to feel peer pressure, especially for things that are bad for you. Unless you are lucky and your peer group pressures you to study, exercise, eat well...yeah, right. It doesn't happen too often, does it?

Count on it: Peers who smoke, drink, and harass others will want you to do the same.

Why do you suppose they want you to participate in these activities?

Because if you don't, you are demonstrating a stronger willpower than they have. You are preparing yourself for a better life, one that they will probably never know. They'd prefer that you share their miserable situation.

Disassociate yourself from such "friends."

You can get involved with activities that make you a better person and prepare you for life. The world is full of possibilities. Instead of destroying yourself, you can spend your time and energies on sports, academic work, learning a new language, volunteer work, reading, and much more.

By the way, would you advise yourself to smoke, drink, and use drugs?

If you wouldn't, why let your peers influence you?

The ugly (really ugly)

Make no mistake. Anyone who asks you (or forces you) to get involved with drugs, violence, gangs, or illegal activity is really damaging your life.

Stay away from such people; they are not really your friends anyway. If you live in a neighborhood where such activities are common, avoiding them is much harder. But you can still do it.

Talk to someone older whom you trust (such as a parent, school counselor, teacher, minister, or rabbi).

To live the good life, you must avoid the ugly influences life throws in your way.

Your opinion of yourself ... or others' opinion of you?

For most teenagers, this one is difficult to handle.

Adults don't usually understand this part of their kids' lives. They forget how important it was to them when they were young. Of course, in a perfect world you wouldn't care about your peers' opinion of you. But in the real world, it's hard not to care about it. Advice from parents to ignore peer pressure sounds pretty hollow.

Why? *Because you are the one experiencing it first hand in school.* You are the one who has to face the pressure, the insults, and the rejection.

So how do you handle people who want to drag you down with them?

Stay out of their way. Get strength in numbers. Make friends with interests similar to yours — some hobby club, sports activity, or charity. And bear this in mind: It's one thing to care about someone's opinion of you (especially if you respect that person). But should you really care about the opinions of people who really don't have your best interest in mind? Should anyone care?

You don't have to do things just to please others.

Declare your independence, and mean it. People will applaud you for it!

Distractions in the Teen Phase

Smoking

Dating

Serious dating with long-term commitments

Television

"Oh, I am so bored, I have nothing to do ..."

Smoking

I have been diagnosed with emphysema. Do you know what that means? I'm 41 years old. From now until I die, I am hooked to an oxygen tank. Wherever I go, the oxygen tank goes with me.

I started smoking when I was 14 because I thought it was cool. My friends smoked, so I smoked. Two of my best friends have been diagnosed with lung cancer. One was smart — he quit before the health problems started.

If you smoke — quit. If you don't, then don't start.
It's addictive, and getting off it is really difficult.

—**Steve, 41, Phoenix, AZ**

How do the tobacco companies get people hooked on cigarettes?

For one thing, tobacco companies aim at teens. They do this by trying to convince them that smoking is "cool." Their commercials show macho men riding horses, or sitting on fence posts with the rugged countryside in the background. They show beautiful women with cigarettes dangling from their mouths. And until the government made them stop, they made advertisements aimed directly at teenagers. These ads are very enticing, and they work. Otherwise, the tobacco companies wouldn't be spending millions of dollars on them.

A casting agent approached a close friend of mine, an accomplished actress. He wanted her to "join a bunch of pretty actresses to go to bars glamorizing smoking."

She refused. It was a very brave thing to do, because she turned down money. But she stuck to her ethics. (Please read the section on being a role model — page 69.)

So what do you do? You could do the same as so many others — light up a cigarette. Well, guess what? More than likely, you'll be hooked for life. The models, the actors, and the advertising agency make money, and the tobacco companies get a lifetime customer (you).

And what does smoking do for you? Does it really make you look cool?

What it really does is ruin your health, stink up your clothes, and blacken your lungs. If you smoke long enough, it could give you emphysema or cancer.

(If after reading this you still want to smoke...hey, it's your life...you get to choose.)

Dating

Don't let it take over your life.

In your teen years, you need to focus on preparing for the realities of life. Although dating plays an important role in interacting with the opposite sex, focusing only on dating is not going to give you the skills you need to live.

Instead of spending your energies on the heartaches and emotional roller coasters that come with relationships, you could spend the time on sports, developing hobbies, additional course work, travel, learning languages, and other activities of your choice. There is plenty of time to pursue relationships after you get settled in your career. In the meantime you can discover for yourself the type of person you are, including your likes and dislikes. Discovering yourself will help you make a better choice when you select a life partner. And it will make you a better life partner, too.

Here are some facts to remember: Most marriages that begin in the teenage years end in divorce. Why? Because neither the boy nor the girl knows what to look for in marriage. Unfortunately, this gets more and more clear as the two grow up and mature. Eventually, the mismatch in their expectations becomes so obvious that the best choice is to separate.

You are not the same person now that you'll be in another ten years or so.

Of course, young couples often have kids, and this complicates things.

Now picture this:

- A young marriage fails.
- They have kids that need care.
- A divorce ensues.
- Either the father or the mother gets primary custody of the kids.
- The courts get involved. Alimony and child-support payments begin.
- On the emotional rebound, the separated spouses remarry or get into other serious relationships, have more kids...and the same miserable story starts again.

Tough thought — look around and see how many of your friends or peers come from families that fit this picture.

Ask yourself this question: "Do I really need these complications when I am in my teens?"

Serious dating with long-term commitments

Before you get seriously involved and consider long-term commitments, here are some things to consider:
- What do I really like about this person? Do we have things in common that we can both enjoy?
- If we drop out of school now to pursue this relationship, what kind of financial stability will we have for the present and the future?
- If we have kids, would I be comfortable with this person as a parent of my child?
- Do we share mutual respect? How does he or she treat me?
- Is he or she responsible and trustworthy?
- Do I see myself spending the rest of my life with this person?

Just look at the Personals section in your local newspaper. Here are some attributes people are looking for in their mate:
- Dependable
- Good personality, attitude
- Mature
- Intelligent
- Open-minded
- Drug-free
- Well educated
- Financially secure
- Caring
- Sincere

How many of these qualities does your partner have?

Most important of all, do you know for sure what you want from your partner? And are you sure that is what he or she has in mind?

Television

How much is enough?

That depends.

If you've finished what you planned for the day — your homework, sports, housework (I must be kidding, right?) — and you have free time and want to relax, then go ahead and watch TV.

Just don't get addicted to TV. Watch it only for what it is worth — *entertainment*.

Remember this: The actors, directors, writers, and others who present the shows are doing it for *their own careers*. **They are making money while you spend your time watching their shows and making them wealthy.**

TV offers you only passive entertainment. By watching TV, you are actually living someone else's life, not your own. Worse, many people let the tube think for

them. After all, you can't really interact with the tube; you can only absorb what it shows. Isn't it far better to spend time thinking on your own or interacting with other people?

Why it is better to spend time either thinking by yourself or interacting with people? The mind is really like a muscle: The more you exercise it (challenge it), the stronger it gets. So if you spend time mulling over thoughts or situations in your mind, you build your ability to think clearly. By spending time interacting with others, you can develop your social skills, enjoy the company of your friends, and learn something new from them.

"Oh, I am so bored, I have nothing to do ..."

(Dealing with free time)

As a teenager, you probably have lots of free time.

If you use this time wisely, you'll see many benefits in the future.

For example, between school terms you could enroll for a course in a foreign language. By learning a language like French, German, Spanish, or Japanese, you could improve your employability immensely. You could also expand your life's possibilities. Just for the fun of it, look at the employment section of your local newspaper and look at the jobs that require a foreign language (or consider it a plus). Some of these jobs send you all over the world, and pay you for it — sometimes very well.

Hear it from 26-year-old Stephanie from Redwood City, CA:

I graduated from college with a Liberal Arts degree. To get an entry into a well-known company, I accepted placement as a temporary employee at $18.00 per hour (about $19,000 per year).

I had taken French as a foreign language and could read and write fluently.

The marketing department was looking for someone with French language skills, and I was at the right place at the right time with just what they were looking for and was hired to do the job. The company hired me with a starting salary of $32,000 per year, plus full benefits. It was the start of a great career and a life of independence.

Would you like to be in a similar situation someday in your life?

Self doubts

If you are average, should you continue to study (or go to college)?

Yes, you should.

You need that certificate that confirms you finished college. Why? Because when you seek employment in a

company, the hiring manager will look for the "Educa-tion" section on your résumé. If you don't have a col-lege degree, you could lose out.

Here's another way to look at this. You are one ap-plicant among many, and even with similar years of experience, a candidate with a degree almost always gets the chance over one without. A degree gives you an edge.

Also consider the following interesting facts from a government survey:

Over a lifetime, a typical *high school graduate* makes $250,000 more than a *high school dropout* does. On the other hand, a typical *college graduate* makes $600,000 more than an average *high school graduate* does over a lifetime. Think about it: If four years of college is worth $600,000 over your lifetime, it comes to $150,000 per college year!

Is there anything else you could do during those years important enough to give up that kind of money?

Apart from the monetary benefit of going to college, a college education contributes to your personal growth. You also make invaluable friends and contacts. Contacts are a great way to get jobs.

More people do better in college than they do in high school. Why? Because in college you can specialize in something that you are interested in and not have to learn a host of subjects, as you do in high school.

Values to Carry You Through Life

Why have values?

Honesty

Courage

Self-discipline

Dependability

Sensitivity

Sense of fairness

Values (revisited)

Why have values?

Your values (dictionary meaning: principles or qualities) determine the kind of person you are. They help you make decisions regarding your relationships with friends, parents, siblings (brothers and sisters), and society in general. Your core values determine how you react to situations that test your character.

For example, suppose you find a wallet or purse on the sidewalk and you decide to open it. Inside you find money, credit cards, and a driver's license. You now have the following choices:

- Do you call the person and let him or her know?
- Do you keep the money and mail back the rest, so the person at least won't have to replace the other items?
- Do you take the money and dump the wallet or purse?
- Do you pocket the cash, use the credit cards to make fraudulent purchases, and dump the rest?

What would you do if you found yourself in the above situation?

Now, lets see how you would conduct yourself.

- If you're the type who feels compassion for others, you'll notify the owner. If you feel that it is not right to keep someone else's belongings, you have honesty and integrity, and you'll return everything.

- If you lack values and believe in "Finders keepers, losers weepers," you will pocket whatever is of use and dump the rest.
- If you really lack values and have dishonest intentions, you could commit fraud by using the unfortunate person's credit cards to order goodies for yourself.

You are the one who decides what values you have. In turn, your values determine how you live your life.

Your values also determine how you treat your boyfriend or girlfriend, brothers, sisters, parents, husband or wife, children, friends, employer, boss, and just about everyone else. *Values are destiny.*

Some of the most important values that define your character are honesty, courage, self-discipline, dependability, sensitivity, and a sense of fairness. These are the building blocks for your life.

Let's look at the importance of each one.

Honesty

Think about the previous example, in which you found someone else's wallet or purse and considered various options. If you're truly honest, you'll resist the temptation to keep the contents, and you'll return everything to the rightful owner. (What would you want someone to do if they found your wallet or purse?)

As you progress through your teen years, the honesty issue extends to greater and greater areas of your life. For example, you might be in a position to cheat on exams, copy someone else's term paper, or cheat on your girlfriend or boyfriend.

Being honest means refusing to lie, steal, or indulge

in activities that you know are not ethical (or, in some cases, legal).

It really takes a lot of courage to stay honest.

Remember this. It takes a long time to build an honest reputation, but it takes only one dishonest action to destroy it.

Courage

Picture this. Your friends are getting high, or vandalizing, or indulging in some other illegal activity. They want you to do the same.

You know it's not the right thing to do.

If you walk away, they'll taunt you, call you a coward, drop you from their group, or even threaten you.

So now you're faced with a situation that requires *courage.*

You know the right thing to do. And to do the right thing, you'll need a lot of courage. You'll have to stand up to them, even if they call you a coward.

Frankly, if you walk away and refuse to join them, *you* are the one with courage. They are the cowards, because they have no self-discipline. They are doing things that you know, and they know, are wrong.

You'll definitely encounter situations requiring courage throughout your life. Some of the tougher decisions will come years from now, so learn courage now.

Self-discipline

Interestingly, you'll need self-discipline not only in your teen years, but throughout your adult life as well.

In your teen years, self-discipline concerns such things as:

- Sticking to your homework schedule instead watching TV or hanging out with friends
- Eating in moderation
- Making friends who are less "cool," who take their studies seriously and want to make something out of their lives
- Not making constant demands on your parents for the latest and greatest clothes, shoes, music, and CDs
- Investing your free time in learning some skill or language
- Planning ahead for your future and not giving in to distractions
- Making your college plans

The better you get at disciplining yourself, the more control you'll have in your life.

Look around you. Do you see adults in financial trouble? You probably do. Or people with no savings, their careers in ruins, working terrible jobs, and enduring a meager existence? In the worst cases, they may live on welfare.

Ask yourself how they got into such a terrible mess.

Most of these people could have avoided their misery by showing some self-discipline. Unfortunately, many adults continue to behave like irresponsible kids and make foolish decisions, such as buying beyond their means, not saving for retirement, and not planning their careers properly. These people are in serious trouble.

The sooner you learn to discipline yourself, the better off you'll be in life.

So just for fun, try a new "trick" the next time you're offered something you know isn't really good for you (chocolate, for example). *Don't take it.* It might bother you at first, but in time you'll get used to disciplining yourself. The more practice you get with self-discipline now, the easier it'll be years later.

Self-discipline is not easy, and it's not always fun. But people who learn to control their urges have better control over their lives. They stay out of trouble and avoid the misery that always seems to follow people who lack self-discipline.

Dependability

To depend means "to place trust or reliance."

Since you probably "depend" on your parents (or guardians), you know the importance of being dependable. So, shouldn't you be the same?

To deserve the reputation of being a dependable person, you need to keep the promises and commitments you make.

For example, you promise to call your mom if you decide to stay out late with your friends.

You forget. Your mom worries about you.

Do you think you'll be considered dependable after that? Probably not. The next time you make a commitment to your mom, she's likely to doubt that you'll follow through on your promise.

The sooner you get the reputation of being dependable, the better off you'll be. Your peers, friends, parents, and teachers will treat you with more respect. You might even start enjoying special privileges; for example, your parents might be more generous with their car, or give you additional freedom. Best of all, they might treat you like an adult.

Interestingly, one of the key attributes that employers look for in prospective employees is dependability.

Acquire this value and you'll really have a head start on everyone else.

Sensitivity

Dictionary meaning — "awareness of the needs and emotions of the others."

Other words with the same meaning are compassion, sympathy, and understanding.

Sensitivity is another quality that takes you far in life. By showing sensitivity or compassion for the feelings or needs of others, you'll be a better person. And other people will see that and respect you for it.

You may encounter situations where your friends make fun of someone weaker, or insult someone of the opposite sex. At such times, you'll need not only sensitivity but also courage to defend the person under attack.

Don't think that you'll be considered a "sissy" if you show sensitivity.

On the contrary, you'll earn a lot of respect from people around you.

Sense of fairness

This is one of the most important values.

Once you get the hang of fairness, your life will be enriched — maybe with money, but definitely in your relationships with friends, family, and with others. It will help you even more later in life, when you work at a career or run your own business.

To get a sense of fairness, you need to have honesty,

courage, self-discipline, and sensitivity — some of the other values we've discussed already.

Think of the following scenario. You're the captain of a sports team and have the authority to select the players. As you fill up the available slots, you are confronted with the following situation:

• Two players are competing for the same spot;
• One of them happens to be a good friend of yours;
• The other happens to be a better player.

As captain of the team, you must choose one of them. It's not an enviable task.

Which player do you select? If you select your friend, you are showing favoritism.

If you select the better player, you are doing what is best for the team. *And you are also showing a sense of fairness.*

Of course, this could come at a price. Your friend might not be your friend anymore, you could be branded a traitor, and your other friends might criticize your decision. But your sense of fairness is more important.

Besides, there are other people to think about besides your own friends and acquaintances. You have the team to think about, and they are depending on you.

Such difficult decisions are bound to confront you throughout your lifetime. Have a sense of fairness and make your decisions accordingly.

Values (revisited)

The importance of values cannot be overstated.

They make you what you are. *They define your character.*

As you go about "raising yourself," get your value system right first. It is your value system that helps you make the right choices as you go through life.

Read books and articles about people with the kinds of values and character you admire. Make them your role models and try to be like them.

As you are confronted with tough decisions that make you choose between right and wrong, think about how your role models would act.

Your Mental and Physical Development

Mental

Physical

Mental

Reading

Congratulations! By now it is obvious that you read, in spite of the easy distractions of TV and radio.

At the very least, reading gives the following benefits:

- Helps you increase your vocabulary
- Gives practice reading and absorbing information
- Gives you a chance to form your own opinion (without bias from radio and TV commentators)

What should you read?

Go to the local library or bookstore and browse through the aisles. You are bound to find some books that interest you. Try to include both fiction and nonfiction in your reading.

Some of the best nonfiction books are titled "How To...." Your local library or bookstore usually has a large selection of such books, especially in the Self-Improvement, Reference, or Psychology section. You could start with books like "How to Improve Your Vocabulary in 30 Days," or "How to Plan for Your Future," or "How to Score Higher Grades." It's surprising how useful these books can be.

Such books often contain recommendations for other books, either in the main part of the book or at the end. I personally have read many of these books. Some of them are classics. They have helped many people (myself included) and motivated us to achieve our dreams and goals.

They might do the same for you.

There are lots of novels, short stories, and other fictional works that are both entertaining and thought provoking.

Tip: Keep a dictionary handy. Get in the habit of using it when you are unsure of the meaning of a word. That's a sure way of improving your vocabulary.

Browsing the Worldwide Web (http://www...)

And while we're on the subject of reading:

If you have access to the worldwide web (WWW), you can spend many entertaining hours there browsing and learning. Go for it! Learn how to research your ideas online and follow the links. The Web can even help you find books to read. For example, there are lots of excellent online bookstores, such as amazon.com and barnesandnoble.com.

Just be careful. Time passes quickly on the Internet, and some people waste a lot of time chasing links from site to site. For these people, the Web is the modern-day TV — not exactly brain food. But with a little care and common sense, you can make it an incredible adventure and a learning experience.

Writing

Write.

Express yourself. Put your thoughts and emotions on paper (or a computer).

Writing can be good for the soul. Through it, you can reduce depression, anger, or pain. It's well known that putting down your frustrations in writing helps to relieve the stress.

Have your parents, a teacher, a good friend, or some other person you respect read what you have written. Try to find someone experienced in writing, and ask that person to evaluate what you have written. He or she could give you a new angle, and make suggestions that could improve the quality of your writing.

Over time you'll develop a writing style that is yours alone. You never know; there may even be a professional writer waiting within you.

Hobbies

Pick up a hobby.

For example, you could be:
- Building model airplanes
- Assembling electronic devices
- Playing with model trains. (Even adults do it!)
- Writing for your school or local community paper
- Learning about different countries, languages, and cultures
- Playing a musical instrument
- Sewing
- Gardening
- Woodworking
- Baking, decorating cakes, etc.

- Collecting shells, insects (dead), stamps, coins
- Drawing or painting
- Playing a sport — tennis, basketball, soccer, hockey, etc.

...and there are dozens of other hobbies that you could enjoy.

Interestingly, you might just find some hobby that turns into a career.

For example, a Professor of Consumer Affairs (clothing) at a university started out with a sewing hobby.

A friend's daughter enjoyed playing the violin. Her ability to play the violin was noticed by a symphony director, and he offered her a position in the orchestra.

Physical

Your physical appearance

Your physical appearance is very important. The first impression you make on others determines what they think of you, and physical appearance determines first impressions. No one likes to admit this, but like it or not, it is true.

No, I am not talking about your appearance in the traditional sense — whether you are fat, thin, tall, short, handsome or beautiful. I am talking about how you carry yourself, and how you show yourself to the world. The impression you make is based on whether

- You look clean or scruffy;
- You stand straight or slouch;
- Your hair is well groomed or dirty;
- You are dressed decently or like a bum.

Maintaining a good physical appearance takes some effort, but it's worth it. If you don't believe me, try an experiment. Wear some formal clothes (suit and tie if you're a guy, formal dress if you're a girl), then walk into a shop, a bank, or a restaurant and observe the way people treat you and talk to you. Then see how they relate to you when you're wearing a shabby jacket, scruffy shoes, and have your shirt half-stuffed into tattered jeans.

For better or for worse, how you dress makes all the difference in the world.

Dieting

(The only information you need to keep your weight in check)

Diet. The word brings shudders to most of us, and yet it is written and talked about more than almost any other subject in the world.

The dictionary meaning of diet is "eating sparingly or eating according to prescribed rules."

"Eating sparingly" sounds similar to "eating moderately" or "eating only what you need." Yet thousands of books are written on dieting that all say pretty much the same thing.

Did you know that for millions of people, a diet is the most difficult thing to follow? It often seems that the very word *diet* releases some chemical in our brains that makes us want food we otherwise wouldn't think of eating. Most people think of a diet as an unattractive, life-restricting thing that is heavy on goals and light on fun. That's why so few people stick to diets.

So the first thing to do is to drop the word *diet* from your vocabulary. Instead, use the long (dictionary) term — **eat appropriately.**

To maintain good health and keep your weight in check, remember the following rule: *Eat 15 times the ideal weight you want to maintain in calories.* For example, if you want to weigh 150 pounds, you should eat 15 x 150, or 2,250 calories per day.

Of course, this is not always easy. Most restaurants serve far more food than the human body needs, so they can justify charging the prices they do. For example, some restaurants serve one pound of pasta per serving.

That alone makes up 800 calories. Then add the sauce, which is about 600 calories. Even if that's all you eat, you've just swallowed about 1,400 calories! Add a cola drink (150 calories) and dessert (another 600 calories), and you've got 2,150 calories. And this is only one meal, perhaps lunch or dinner. Add what you've eaten the rest of the day, and see how the calories add up.

So here is an easy policy to follow: Don't deny yourself anything; *just use common sense.*

Instead of eating the main course by yourself, share it with someone else. If you are eating alone, stop eating midway and take the rest with you for later.

Also, eat slowly. It takes about 15 to 20 minutes for your stomach to signal your brain that you are full. Most of us tend to eat fast, so we are stuffed by the time the stomach signals the brain.

Not all foods are created equal. Even when different food items have the same number of calories, they can still have different percentages of fat. That makes a *big* difference. It's well known that the body stores calories from fatty foods more efficiently than calories from fat-free foods. For example, even if a cantaloupe has the same number of calories as a scoop of ice cream, your body stores the fat from the ice cream more easily than the carbohydrate in the cantaloupe. So knowing the calorie count isn't enough. Know what your food is made of, and adjust your eating habits accordingly.

Unless you have incredible willpower, don't bother carrying a pocket calculator with a calorie chart. It's a pain, and when you don't follow it you end up feeling guilty. Use common sense instead. Let's face it, you probably know very well what's fattening and what isn't.

Personally, I wish I had followed this advice earlier so I wouldn't have to fight the weight battle now. Of course, my parents advised me on this — but hey, who listens to them anyway? Now that I'm "raising myself," I follow a simple rule: I eat half (or less) of what I would normally eat. For example, when I eat desserts, chocolates, cheeses, nuts, or cookies, I have only half as much as I *think* I want. (Once I get used to this lifestyle, I'll reduce the intake even more.)

Working out (exercising)

Exercise. It's another word that gives people a chill.

Next to dieting, it's the most talked-about and written-about subject in our society today.

As with the "D" word, the "E" word badly needs demystifying. The dictionary meaning is "physical fitness." Like that one better?

By exercising, you maintain physical fitness. By being physically fit, you get a world of benefits — better blood circulation, improved digestion, a general healthy feeling, resistance to diseases, sharper mental abilities, and many other benefits. Most important, by keeping fit you keep your heart in shape. And needless to say, exercise has the added advantage of burning calories. That means you can eat that chocolate sundae (half of it, of course) without feeling bad.

When you burn calories through exercise or a physical activity, it does not end there. By working off those calories, you increase your basal metabolic rate — the rate at which your body burns calories while resting.

Contrary to popular belief, maintaining good fitness is not particularly difficult or complicated. Your exercise program could be as simple as climbing stairs, walking for a mile or two, or participating in a sport you enjoy.

Where can you go to stay physically fit? You can go the cheap way or the expensive way:

- *Cheap:* Use public facilities for jogging, tennis, running, hiking, and other physical activities. Join a sports team at school.
- *Expensive:* Join a health club or gym.

Indulge in a sport or activity that you enjoy — biking, dancing, walking with a friend, etc.

Do it any way you wish.

Remember: You are doing this for yourself. Don't be too impressed by some athlete on television. What worked for him or her might not work well for you. Find something that you enjoy doing. As long as it gives you a good workout and makes you feel better, you can ignore advice from the media.

Heads-up on excess weight loss ...

The way you treat your body now determines how you'll feel when you're fully mature.

When you're a teenager, your body is still developing and growing. It needs a wide variety of nutrients, which can only come from a balanced mix of food types. Don't deprive yourself of these nutrients. It'll affect the way your body develops — hair, eyes, skin, height, weight, etc.

Eating less than what you need may make you feel tired and sleepy, and affect your performance at school (concentration).

A good mix of food and physical activity will do wonders for your physical development. And that has a big impact on the quality of your life.

When in doubt about nutrition, seek the advice of a physician or some other knowledgeable adult. Don't just consult your peers; their knowledge could be inaccurate or incomplete.

Raising Yourself —
If You Are a Male

Role model (yes, you)

Looking cool may lead to a not-so-hot future

Are you a gentleman or a jerk?

Sex and you (no, not gender, but the *act of sex*)

Role model (yes, you)

Someday you'll be a role model for someone else — perhaps for your brother, your sister, a neighborhood kid, or (in the future) your own children. That's a big responsibility.

Chances are, you currently have a role model that you look up to. Consider the qualities this person has. Write them down. Figure out what it will take for you to become a positive role model for someone else.

Think about it. If you don't have your own act together, how can you expect others to look up to you?

And if someone does look up to you, wouldn't you like to be worthy of it? Isn't it far better to have a positive influence on others than a negative influence?

The qualities of a good role model are:

- Integrity (honesty)
- Respect for others
- Commitment
- Charity
- Responsibility
- Excellence in work
- Leadership
- Vision (ability to look ahead)

If you are involved in drugs, gangs, vandalism, and violence, you run two risks. One is that no one will look up to you at all. The other is that someone will look up to you, and be destroyed along with you. Either way, society has very little tolerance for people who engage in criminal activity. It is bound to land you, and the people you influence, in deep trouble.

Looking cool may lead to a not-so-hot future

Coolness is an issue that almost everyone faces at some time or another.

The desire for coolness is usually based on vanity, which is a deadly human weakness. The search for coolness often leads to destructive behavior such as smoking, drinking, and using drugs. The antidote for self-destructive coolness is humility. By "humility" I don't mean self-hatred or masochism; I mean exactly the opposite. True humility is actually a form of self-confidence. It's a personal attitude that doesn't seek peer approval, and refuses to give in to pressure or popular fashion. It means living life wisely and with a clear head.

Humility is not something that everyone has naturally.

It comes over time, and if it comes too late it can be devastating. Most "cool" people experience a painful stripping of coolness later in life. As the years go by, they watch the other kids mature and succeed, gaining self-confidence, wealth, independence, and respect.

Hanging out and looking "cool" might win a few friends now. But one day you could end up hanging out at the corner looking for day jobs. How "cool" will you feel then?

Are you a gentleman or a jerk?

It's another one of those choices you make as you pass through the teen years.

You can already see how some of your peers treat others — including the opposite sex, people with disabilities, people of different races, and other living creatures such as pets.

Some people consider it "cool" to make sarcastic remarks, or to comment on others' physical appearance. But the impression such people really make is almost always negative. Almost everyone considers them jerks. When anyone tries to make friends through rudeness, don't fall for it.

Even if you cannot influence your peers who display "jerk-like" behavior, you can distance yourself from them. People will most likely associate you with these peers even if you do not display the same behavior.

Think of how much better it will be for your self-esteem if people around you consider you a decent, kind person. You'll have an enviable reputation.

Remember, "You don't get taller standing on other people."

Sex and you (no, not gender, but the act of sex)

The act of sex without protection can be deadly. It's not just the girl's problem if she gets pregnant. It's yours too. You too have a responsibility, and if you think you can walk away, think again. There are laws now that will hold you accountable for your actions.

An unwanted pregnancy can significantly affect your life. Suddenly your responsibility will triple — you will need to provide for your partner, the child, and yourself.

Apart from getting your partner pregnant, you risk getting sexually transmitted diseases. And of course, if you get AIDS, there is no cure.

Raising Yourself — If You Are a Female

One extremely important thing you can do that men can't

Life has no guaranties

Sex and you (no, not the gender, but the *act of sex*)

Drinking (and/or drugs) and dating don't mix

Dealing with boys and their abuse (verbal or physical)

Career stereotyping

One extremely important thing you can do that men can't

Get pregnant.

No matter how badly a guy might mess up his life, he can't mess it up by getting pregnant.

On the other hand, you can.

If it happens, and you decide to keep the baby, there's no guarantee that the father will be around to help. You may find yourself responsible for raising the child, providing education, and instilling values. Whether you do it by yourself, with the support of family, and/or with the child's father, raising a child is a heavy burden. A recently published study shows that single moms are eight times more likely to live in poverty than married couples.

OK, life is unfair.

So why make it tougher by stacking the odds against yourself?

(Note: To understand the challenges that you could face as a teen, read the book *Reviving Ophelia* by Mary Pipher, published by Ballantine Books.)

Life has no guaranties
(Be prepared to take care of yourself.)

Even if you dream of having a husband who will support you financially for the rest of your life, you need to prepare for the unexpected.

Common thought (delusion): I will marry someone rich. He will take care of me forever.

Reality #1: Unless you have a good education, plus the sophistication and social skills that come with it, rich men aren't likely to be interested, no matter how beautiful you are. In the real world, wealthy men (and women) tend to marry people on their own level. Fairy tales of rich, handsome men marrying poor Cinderella come true only in the movies.

Reality #2: Many rich guys get bored with material possessions, and chances are that's exactly how he will treat you – especially when it dawns on him that you're after his money. For him, you could be a mere plaything, easy to get rid of once he gets tired of you.

Reality #3: Even if you manage to marry a rich man for his money, what will make the marriage work? How long could you really live and sleep with a man you don't really love? And make no mistake; sooner or later, the guy will figure out why you married him. If he has any self-respect at all, he'll divorce you.

Why would you want to place yourself in that position?

As a new divorcee, will you be able to give up the expensive tastes you formed shopping at his expense? Would you be ready to deal with the sudden change in your status? After all, the friends you make as his wife will probably be his originally. And they'll probably be loyal to him, not you.

Perhaps most importantly, will you be able to overcome the feeling of being dumped? Can you come out of a divorce, pick up the pieces, and move on? Will you have something to fall back on so your mind won't be occupied with the pain of the breakup?

You owe it to yourself to think of these things before getting into such a situation.

There's just no substitute for getting the education and skills you need for a good, high-paying job. For one thing, it will do wonders for your self-esteem. If you're in a bad relationship, you'll be able to leave without worrying about supporting yourself. You'll declare your independence, and you'll never have to stay in a relationship because you can't survive on your own. Keep in mind — successful people are like magnets, attracting other successful people.

Additionally, by acquiring education, skills, and good self-esteem, you will make an equal partner in the future relationship. Your partner can rely on your support to acquire new skills, start a business, or take risks to improve your lifestyle.

Sex and you (no, not gender, but the *act of sex*)

Here are some things you should keep in mind:

If you're having sex with your boyfriend, the chances are good that he's done the same with someone else. You have no idea what disease he might have picked up from someone else.

If you get AIDS ... well, you know that there is no cure for AIDS.

If you get pregnant, do you know for sure that he'll be around to support you and the baby? Assuming he's in a position to support you financially, are you ready to have a child? Do you know what it takes to care for and bring up a child? Have you spent a day with someone who has an infant and verified that you are ready to take on similar responsibilities?

It's wise to keep the worst scenario in mind. If you get pregnant, your boyfriend dumps you, and you have to leave home, will you be ready to raise the child on your own? Are you finished "raising yourself"?

If you plan to have sex, insist on your partner using

a condom for your own sake. But be aware of, and be prepared for, the consequences of your actions if that protection fails.

Drinking (and/or Drugs) and dating Don't Mix

It's a known fact that alcohol and drugs can dull your senses and makes you (and your partner) reckless. What you normally wouldn't do while sober, you might do while under the influence. The solution is simple: To avoid situations you'll regret later on, *stay sober in the first place.*

However confident you are of your ability to take care of yourself, you may not be strong enough when it matters the most — when you are under the influence and someone is hitting on you for sex.

One mistake under the influence could **cost you immensely ... AIDS, an unwanted pregnancy,** a car wreck, or some other disaster.

Dealing with jerks (boys) and their abuse (verbal or physical)

No one has the right to abuse you — verbally or physically.

Verbal abuse can consist of making comments about your appearance, your family, your grades, your intelligence, your physical attributes, or any other thing you're sensitive about. Such verbal abuse occurs sometimes in school hallways or other public places where boys hang out.

Physical abuse occurs whenever a boy touches you against your wishes. One common way physical abuse happens is in boyfriend/girlfriend relationships. For example, if your boyfriend hits you or shoves you, that is physical abuse. Next to murder, the most severe (and criminal) form of physical abuse is rape, which can happen on a date or even at a party.

You need to stand up for your rights.

If you are experiencing any abuse (verbal or physical), talk to someone you trust, such as your parents, a teacher, a minister, a rabbi, or a school counselor. You are not snitching (telling on your abuser) if you take action for your own safety.

Be aware that if your school fails to take action on your complaints, it can be held liable if you pursue legal action. Jenny (identity changed) was experiencing verbal abuse from the boys in her school. They called her names like "slut," made comments on her bust size, her hair, her thighs, and other physical attributes. They abused and harassed her about anything they could.

She complained to the teachers. They took no action.

Jenny eventually stopped going to school, to avoid the boys. She took her parents into her confidence and they spoke to the school authorities. The school staff trivialized the whole situation.

Jenny's parents sought legal help and sued the school.

The court ruled in favor of Jenny and her family. The school had to pay Jenny several hundred thousand dollars, and her tormentors were expelled from school. Justice was served.

If you are experiencing abuse, speak to an older person you trust. Such a person might help you put the situation into perspective, and help you deal with it.

Career Stereotyping

There is a career for you in engineering, math, sciences, and other disciplines that are usually dominated by males. Don't let society dictate what career you should follow. You need to decide what is suitable for yourself.

If you have the aptitude for science, math, computer science, or engineering, pursue it.

Unfortunately, parents often do disservice to their daughters by excluding them from so-called "boys' activities" — working on the car, using tools, configuring the computer, programming the electronics in the house (VCR, TV, stereo equipment, and so on). Moms tend to involve their daughters in shopping, watching soap operas, prettying themselves, etc.

Be assertive. If you don't get equal access to the home computer, demand it.

You can't afford to take a back seat to activities that are gender neutral.

Don't limit yourself to the stereotypical jobs that are associated with women, such as receptionist, administrative assistant, nurse, teacher, and day care. These tend to be lower-paying jobs.

Go for careers such as medicine, law, engineering, and business. And who knows... President of the United States?

Recommended reading: *What Color is Your Parachute?* by Richard Nelson Bolles, published by Ten Speed Press.

Career Options

Hey, I want one of those glamorous careers

You can have your cake and eat it too

Career choices for the rest of us

Where will the jobs be in the future?

What are your interests?

What if you are not sure?

Hey, I want one of those glamorous careers
(Sports, music, acting, modeling, etc.)

Most of us dream of being rich and famous. In many ways, it's the American dream. A successful career in sports, rock music, Hollywood movies, or modeling is the fantasy of millions.

Unfortunately, it's a long shot. Only a handful make the cut.

For every kid who makes it as a basketball star in the NBA, there are many thousands of kids playing in high schools and on street corners, hoping to do the same thing. And there are only a few who make it. The same goes for acting. Most actors are completely unknown by anyone but the Hollywood unemployment offices.

Here are some qualities that are necessary to make it big in any of these glamorous careers:
- **Passion** ... to succeed
- **Faith** ... in yourself, even when others may be doubting it
- **Practice** ... lots of it
- **Self-discipline** ... willingness to say "no" to distractions
- **Decisiveness** ... ability to make one and stick by it
- **Enthusiasm** ... keeping your spirits up even though you may suffer setbacks
- **Persistence** ... not giving up at the first sign of failure or defeat

If you have these qualities, then go ahead and pursue your dream. Others have done it and succeeded. Just look at Leonardo DiCaprio.

Even so, it would help immensely to take a **reality check** now and then. That way you can cut your losses and move to another option before you invest all your resources — time *and* money — and come up empty-handed.

The smart ones don't give up their dreams, but they also plan for their future. In short, they don't put all their eggs in one basket. They have an alternate plan, in case their best hopes fizzle. That's not cowardice; it's being smart.

Ask yourself the following question: "Do I have what it takes to be successful at a glamorous career?" If the answer is "yes," go for it.

But don't burn your bridges.

You can have your cake and eat it too

Steve was smart.

Nowadays, he works out at an expensive health club. He was a star basketball player in high school, so he decided to go for fame and fortune as a basketball player. Even so, he knew back then what a long shot it was. So in addition to playing basketball, he concentrated on getting his education and preparing for an alternate career.

Today he not only enjoys sports at the health club, but also heads the marketing department at a well-known computer company. Yes, he followed his dream of becoming basketball star in the NBA, and it didn't work out. But he has nothing to regret.

Contrast this to Gary...

Gary wanted to be a professional tennis player, so he devoted himself to this alone. He lagged behind academically, and learned no useful skills in his spare time. Yet despite his best attempts, the competition in the tennis circuit was just too fierce. He wasn't able to win enough tournaments to make a living, much less get rich.

What price did he pay? Because he focused only on tennis, a large chunk of his life passed him by, and he made no progress anywhere else. Now he teaches tennis and barely makes enough to pay his rent.

What kind of a lifestyle can he expect?

You pay a price for the decisions you make. The decisions you make now will determine your education, career, health, and lifestyle. Think what your decisions will cost you in the long term, and make them knowingly.

Career choices for the rest of us

Here are some broad career categories:
- Agriculture and Forestry
- Law Enforcement and Protective Services
- Recreation and Hospitality
- Education and Academia
- Business, Finance, and Related Fields
- Government and Law
- Sales and Marketing
- Nonprofit Agencies and Social Sciences
- Natural Sciences
- Personal and Commercial Services
- Manufacturing
- Transportation
- Health and Medicine
- Building, Construction, and Mining
- Engineering and Computers
- Telecommunications

...and countless other possibilities.

These categories contain many diverse subcategories. For example, under Health and Medicine, there are doctors (MDs), registered nurses (RNs), respiratory therapists, psychiatric technicians, physical therapists, audiologists, and dozens more.

Where will the jobs be in the future?

Look at the newspaper and check out the employment section of the classifieds.

A safe bet:

- Technology — especially jobs related to computers: programmer, systems analyst, application engineer, technical writer, technical trainer, customer support, system administrator, and dozens of other technology-related jobs
- Health Services — doctors, nurses, lab assistants, and related jobs
- Professional Services — attorneys, financial advisors, social workers, sales executives, analytical services, materials management, human resources
- Support Services — maid service, gardening service, plumbing, electrical, water-proofing
- Management Positions — thousands of positions for experienced managers
- Retail — lots of positions in department stores, grocery stores, electronic/computer stores

The newspapers also predict and publish the trends for the future.

Some of the jobs mentioned above will fall in the lower-paying category. The higher-paying jobs will require you to learn skills either in a college or through experience. Select your career based on your aptitudes and interests.

What are your interests?

Think about the kind of career you'd like to have. Although it's not absolutely necessary to figure this out ahead of time, getting some ideas now could be an advantage. It could give you a head start preparing for your career.

Suppose, for example, that you have an interest or aptitude in biology. You could get a summer intern job in a local biotech company or in a laboratory at a local university. Seeing what the work is like could help you decide if you like it enough to make a career out of it.

Sometimes it's difficult to make a career choice based on ability alone. You may be interested in a particular career and pursuing it may give you better job satisfaction. However, it could pay less than the career you have the aptitude for. For example, lets say your passion is tennis and you want to be a tennis coach, while your aptitude is in science. You'd probably have a better income pursuing science than coaching tennis. The choice will be yours to make.

Interestingly, to take the example of tennis versus science, you can have your cake and eat it too. You could always get into science but pursue your tennis coaching interest on the weekends and evenings.

Unfortunately, a lot of teenagers don't venture into the computer industry, thinking (falsely) that a degree in Computer Science is necessary to qualify for any computer job. Interestingly, lots of jobs in the computer industry require only a limited knowledge of computers. A job like that could help you decide if the computer industry is right for you.

You could also ask your school counselor if "career potential" testing is available. These tests could help determine what jobs would be most suited to your interests.

Whatever the career you're interested in, there is probably a way to investigate it for yourself by getting a related job.

What if you're not sure?

No problem here.

Lots of people take many years to figure out what they really want to do with their lives. In an informal survey of people fresh out of college, 7 out of 10 people had no idea what career to pursue. However, a degree, no matter what the subject, still means your potential earning power is increased.

So don't worry about your uncertainty. Some teenagers know for sure, while others work various jobs before discovering, what they really want.

Fact of the matter is — you need a job (money) to survive.

If you're currently not sure about which career to choose, the best way to use your time is to work toward some degree, one that could get you a job. As you mature, and you begin to realize what kind of career you want, you can change direction as needed.

But in the meantime, don't let indecision make you inactive. Always be working on something, even if you're not sure it's the thing you'll finally want.

Would you hire yourself?

Think about it. Would you?

Do you know what employers look for in prospective employees?

Try this:

- **Appearance** — As an employee, you'll be representing the company. If you have purple hair, a ring in your tongue, visible tattoos, or slovenly dress, your job prospects will sink fast — unless you're applying for a job with a rock group or a music store.
- **Attitude** — This is a big one too. Employers look for employees with positive, winning, can-do attitudes and a passion for their work.
- **A strong work ethic** — Responsible and dependable behavior.
- **Communication skills** — Both written and verbal. Many candidates turn in résumés with spelling and grammatical errors. Such résumés go immediately to the "circular file" (the trash can).

Other attributes employers watch for: manners, etiquette, personal hygiene (absence of body odor), verbal skills, and friendliness.

Understanding Money

Money 101

What is debt?

Savings and investments

Money 101

Let's face it, you need money.

To get it, you will need to earn it.

How much you need depends on where you live, your expenses, the size of your family, and many other factors. (See page 17 at the beginning of this book.)

How much you earn depends on your education, your skills, and how much your parents can help. (Of course, it also depends on how much ambition you have, and how committed you are to success.)

You need to earn money, not only for your day-to-day expenses, but also to save for the future. Savings are important. Even animals save. A squirrel knows (thanks to nature) that it's hard to find food in the winter months. The squirrel stashes food so it can eat when food is hard to find.

As a human being, you can learn a thing or two from the animal kingdom. *Savings are important.* They give you staying power. For example, suppose you hate your job, or your job is unstable. If you're fired or you decide to quit, you'll have no income. Who will pay for your day-to-day living expenses?

Unless you have parents or someone else to bail you out, you'll need your savings. You can't always run to your parents for help. They have their own share of expenses, and may not have enough to help you. You have to become financially independent some day.

So you need savings.

But before we talk further about savings, lets look at something really important — *staying out of debt.*

What is debt?

Simply put, debt is what you owe someone else (a friend, your parents, or banks).

You get into debt when you don't have enough to pay for what you buy, or when you don't want to pay money to buy it outright.

Here's another, simpler way to look at it. *You get into debt when you spend more than you earn.*

It's really simple to get into debt — thanks to all the people (banks, private lenders, other lending institutions) that want to lend you money. Ever wonder why your parents receive dozens of advertisements from credit companies, asking them to sign up for new credit cards?

Do you think these companies are doing it out of the goodness of their hearts? No way!

They want you to borrow money (and get into debt) because then you'll have to pay them *interest* (lots of it). Interest is money that banks make you pay when you borrow. It's extra money (a percentage) that you must pay, over and above the money you borrow.

Why do you think the banks are trying so hard to get you to borrow their money? You might think, "Yeah, sure, I'll borrow it. But I'll pay it back too." Unfortunately, it isn't quite so easy. The banks are betting that, because you need the money in the first place, you'll continue needing it for other things, *and won't have the discipline to pay it back.* That way, you'll continue to pay their interest charges.

The terrible thing about debt is that it tends to grow and grow. People who think they'll borrow just a little often end up borrowing a lot. As their debts grow, they almost become slaves to the lenders. Does that sound familiar? It should. In lots of ways, debt can be like an addiction to drugs, tobacco, or alcohol.

But before you think borrowing and paying interest is always bad, lets look at the concept of *good debt* and *bad debt.*

Good debt is money you borrow for a good purpose — buying a house, starting a business, or getting an education. These things can make you richer in the long run.

Bad debt is borrowing money for consumer items such as stereos, clothes, shoes, entertainment, dining out, and other consumer items. These things just drain your money away.

Why the distinction between good debt and bad debt?

Remember: Being in debt means you're paying others for using their money. For that reason, you should only borrow money (and pay the interest) for things you *really* need.

For example, most credit card companies charge around 18% per year in interest. If you borrow $1,000 on your card, the math works out like this:

- Annual interest charges of 18% on $1,000 come to $180 per year.
- $180 divided by 12 months is $15 per month in interest.
- The bottom line: You owe the credit card company $1,000, plus $15 per month until you pay them back.
- Even if you pay off your $1,000 debt six months later, you'll pay $1,000 plus $90, for a grand total of $1,090.

Think about it. You just paid out $90, and you got *nothing* for it! It's a lousy deal.

To stay out of debt, ask yourself one simple question before you buy anything: "Do I *need* it or do I *want* it?"

If you want it, ask yourself honestly why you want it. If you think you need it, do the same. The answer might save you some money.

For example, a certain sporting goods company introduces a new air-filled shoe. The product is heavily advertised, and a sports star endorses it. Your friends rush out and buy the shoes, which cost $150 per pair.

Now think. Do you want the shoes, or do you need them?

Some important facts you need to keep in mind as you develop your spending habits:

- Advertisers have only one purpose in mind. They want you to buy what they have to sell. To put it bluntly, they want to transfer money from your pocket into their pockets.
- When advertisers want you to buy something, they use every trick.

- Typical tricks used by advertisers include glamor, image, endorsements, and (of course!) *sex*.

As we discussed earlier, tobacco companies are notorious for targeting teenagers as new smokers. Do they care about your health? No way!

They use pretty women and handsome men to convince you that smoking is cool, or that smoking will somehow give you sex appeal. But do you really believe, even for a minute, that smoking will make you look sexy? Smoking does just the opposite; it blights your life. Your health suffers, your body reeks of cigarette smoke, your teeth are stained...so where is the sex appeal? *Chances are that by the time you separate hype from reality, you'll be addicted.*

Incredibly, many people go into debt to support their nicotine addiction, which can cost hundreds of dollars per month. And all because they let the advertisers get under their skins.

So before some slick ad campaign cons you into buying something, think a little. And before you borrow money to buy something, think even harder.

Other ways you can get taken:

Buying consumer items on a "low monthly payments" plan. You could very well end up paying twice the price just by falling for a pay-by-the-month plan. Think about it from the store's point of view. Why would they let you use something for free? Surely they *have* to get their investment back for the item they just sold you. And the best way to do it is to make you pay hefty interest on the item you bought.

Here are some smart shopping strategies you can use:

Unless you absolutely need it right away, wait a little

before buying (remember, if something is worth having, it's worth waiting for).

Chances are, with time you'll really be sure you want the item in the first place. Go to one of those used sports equipment shops and see for yourself the large quantities of unused items sold back to the store at heavily discounted prices. (The stores mark up the prices and resell the products to others at a hefty profit.)

The prices for electronic items such as computers, CD/DVD players, and TVs continue to drop. Unless you need the item in a hurry (for a gift or a school project), you're much better off waiting. One of the biggest advantages of waiting is that you might get something better for a lower price.

As you start working, you'll realize that earning money is not easy, and that life has surprises and shocks in store. You need to save money. And you need to stay out of debt.

Savings and investments

You should approach money with one question uppermost in mind: "Will I control my money, or will money control me?"

Interesting question. Think about it.

If something happens to your job or some emergency requires a chunk of money, savings give you reserves to tide you over. But if you don't have savings and you need money urgently, you'll have to borrow and pay interest. You could land in an ugly mess if you borrow money and find you can't pay it back. This could ruin your credit rating, making it very difficult to borrow later for a house, a car, or some other necessity.

So it's critical that you learn to save.

You don't have to wait until you're on your own to start saving. If you receive an allowance, you can decide — right now — to start putting some of it aside as savings.

Reward yourself for saving. When you find the self-discipline to put some money aside, go ahead and buy something for yourself (without dipping into your savings, of course).

The next step after savings is investing. Although you might not be ready yet to invest money, you do need to understand what it means and how it affects your finances in the long run.

Investing is putting money into real estate or securities such as stocks and bonds. The main purpose is to earn *interest*, *dividends*, and *capital appreciation*.

- We've already discussed interest — it's money *you* pay to *others* when you borrow from them. But others will pay *you* interest if you lend *them* money. A good way to lend money is to buy bonds. A bond is a document that says someone (a borrower) owes you money, and must pay you interest.
- Dividends, which you usually earn by owning stocks, are a bit like interest. A stock is a certificate that says you own part of a company. Sometimes it entitles you to some of the company's profits, which the company pays you as dividends.
- Capital appreciation happens when stocks, bonds, real estate, or other securities increase in value after you buy them. For example, even if a stock does not pay dividends, it could still go up in value.

Of course, all investments have some risk, and some

investments are riskier than other investments. For example, some bonds (known as *junk bonds*) pay high rates of interest compared to other bonds. Junk bonds have a higher risk. Some people have made a lot of money with junk bonds, and others have lost. So you have to be careful, and learn all you can before investing.

The biggest reason to invest is simple: It's the only way your money will grow. If you keep $1,000 under your mattress, then after 15 years you'll still have $1,000 under your mattress. And it probably won't be worth as much.

On the other hand, if you put that money in a regular savings account earning 5% compound interest, then your money grows to $2,117 in those same 15 years.

So which is better, putting money under your mattress or in an investment?

Of course, the explanations above are a bit simplified. There are many kinds of investments, each with a different set of rules. As time goes on, you'll learn what the differences are and which investments are right for you. You just have to keep an open mind and remember that investments play an important role in how you manage your money.

Reality Check (Revisited)

Are parents necessary?

> *When I was a boy of fourteen, my father was so ignorant I could hardly stand to have the old man around. But when I got to be around twenty-one, I was astonished at how much the old man had learned in seven years.*
>
> *— Mark Twain*

Are parents necessary?

Yes, they are. And not just for paying for your clothes, music CDs, and pocket money.

By this time, perhaps, you've realized that "raising yourself" is not a simple task. You are not ready yet to face the harsh realities of the world outside the shelter of your parents.

So what are they good for?

They can offer you foresight (actually hindsight, but foresight sounds more visionary and glamorous).

Your parents have been there and done that. They have learned, either first hand or from their own peers, the consequences of decisions made in the teen years.

In addition to offering you advice based on personal experience, they offer you a home, support, and unconditional love. They want you to have the best possible life — perhaps something they themselves didn't have while growing up.

If Only I Could Be a Teenager Again ...

(...and what would I do differently)

You can learn from:
- your parents
- your teachers
- your peers
- books, magazines, and other media
- mistakes that you make
- *mistakes that someone else makes*

One of the best ways to learn is to learn from mistakes others make.

I'm not suggesting that you must never make any mistakes at all. On the contrary, you'll have to take some risks, including calculated risks where you know ahead of time what the worst outcome could be. And your decisions won't always be good.

If you're not sure, ask your parents (or any other older person you respect) about the possible outcome of your decision. Chances are that he or she will know the answer, not because of any crystal ball but because of a lifetime of experience.

Here are some **regrets and experiences** people shared with me when I asked them the following question: "If you could be a teenager again, what would you do differently?"

Drugs

I wish I had never tried drugs.

I was hanging out with friends who did drugs and just for the fun of it, I decided to try it. From that point on, my life went downhill. The first time you only need a little to get high. But as your body adjusts, you start needing more to get the same level of high.

I progressed from smoking weed to speed, LSD, and cocaine.

The turning point came when one of my friends died from an overdose ...

I finally turned to my family to help me get out of the drug addiction.

— *Cathy, 21, Sacramento, CA*

I refused to do drugs.

I knew the dangers of doing drugs and decided to exercise some self-discipline when it came to making a choice between taking and not taking drugs.

I would advise you to do the same. Nobody can make you do drugs. It is your choice.

Don't do it. I am glad I did not. I have not wasted any money, done damage to my health or lost any time to an addiction that is very hard to overcome.

— *Xavier, 18, Dallas, TX*

I sold drugs to fund my drug habit. I made a lot of money.

But I lived in constant fear of being arrested or getting shot. It's for real. You can get killed selling drugs. People who deal in drugs are in it for money. They don't care what happens to you or to them. Most of the time they are stoned out of their senses and make bad decisions without any thought — like shooting you if you have crossed them.

Stay away from drugs — doing them or selling them.

—Andy, 23, Los Angeles, CA

The next morning I did not remember who I had sex with, since I was stoned.

You too can lose complete control of your senses under the influence of drugs or alcohol and do something like that and really pay the price — AIDS, unwanted pregnancy or some other sexually transmitted disease (STD).

Please learn from my mistakes, don't do drugs or consume so much alcohol that you don't have control on your actions.

—Michelle, 16, San Jose, CA

Dating, relationships, and pregnancy

I would not let dating take over my life. I did nothing but think of my boyfriend, day in and day out. I was obsessed with pleasing him. I wasted years and years and ironically, as we grew older, our interests changed and we drifted apart. If I could do it again,

I would focus on my future and limit dating to free time after school, homework, and sports.
                    —Jennifer, 27, San Jose, CA

I was pregnant at 15. I was careless, and on a date that resulted in sex, I got pregnant. I did not think it would happen to me.

Well, I was wrong. My life is changed forever.

I had dreamt of going to college, traveling the world, but now I am busy being a parent.

Now I realize, I am not ready for such a responsibility. I should have waited.
                    —Cynthia, 19, Long Beach, CA

Don't think having a child will give you the love you are looking for or improve your relationship with your boyfriend. You might drift apart and he may not be ready to give you the support you need to raise the child.
                    —Camille, 20, New York, NY

I had sex just so I would no longer be a virgin. It's OK not to have sex. Don't give in to pressure just because others are doing it.

Now I wish I hadn't had sex just so I could brag about it. You never know, you might also get AIDS or some other disease.
                    —Xiana, 18, Phoenix, AZ

I had a child while in the teens. I really shouldn't have got into this mess — no education, no skills, working in low-paying jobs. I made a poor decision, which is costing me dearly. I wish I had waited until I had a strong relationship and my partner and I were ready for the child.

Please think before getting pregnant. Your decision will forever change your life.

—Stephanie, 26, Orlando, FL

I had sex with my boyfriend because I thought that would make him love me more. But really, that's not what builds the relationship. We are not even together anymore.

—Cynthia, 17, Las Vegas, NV

Abuse and sexual harassment

I saw lots of girls in my school harassed by the most popular boys in school — usually, the basketball and football players.

For the 'star' players, using girls for sex and discarding them was a status symbol. It is cool to hang out with the well-known boys in school, but you'd better know their intention before you get into a situation where they can take advantage of you sexually. Because most of the times, their intent is to use you for sex or to show their power by being abusive to you.

—Jack, 22, Orlando, FL

I was abused by a boy in my class. At first, I thought it was somehow my fault and did not have the courage to stand up for myself.

I was afraid that I would be branded a snitch, but really, no one has the right to harass you. I finally decided to talk to my parents. They spoke to the class teacher and the principal. The school authorities called the boy's parents and told them the behavior must stop. It did.

I am glad I spoke up. If you are being abused, speak to your parents, your teacher or the school counselor. Don't let somebody abuse you.

—Andrea, 20, Oakland, CA

Parents

I shut my parents out of my life when I was in my teens. As a 35-year-old, I look to my parents for advice. I regret I never listened to them as a teenager. I missed out on advice that could have significantly improved my life.

—Mark, 35, Los Angeles, CA

I thought I knew so much then. Now I realize how little I knew.

—John, 45, Phoenix, AZ

I'm 28 years old and back living with my parents. They took me back with open arms. Life is really tough and I squandered all the chances I had while growing up, because I thought I knew better.

—Lisa, 28, San Francisco, CA

Careers in sports

I thought I would make it big in football. I was on top only until I was in college. I never made the big leagues. Now I work in a health club at $10 per *hour while I know that I have the capacity to do better. But why would anyone hire me over a more skilled person? If I had known better, I would have prepared for an alternate career.*

—Steve, 29, Santa Clara, CA

How Do You Measure Success?

As an adult you will probably measure success in the following ways:
- Did you achieve the things you wanted, or were you afraid to venture out and take risks?
- Do you have family, and can you count on one another?
- Do you have close friends with whom you can share memories, laugh, and have fun?
- Is your mind so rich with thoughts that you are not afraid of being by yourself?
- Are you mentally and physically fit?
- Did you volunteer your time to make a difference in someone else's life?
- Were you a responsible citizen, concerned enough to take care of the environment?
- Did you travel to other countries and make new friends?
- Did you (or will you) take care of your parents as they grow old and need your help?

• Can you say you lived your life to the fullest?

So think now what you want the answers to the above questions to be and how you plan to achieve them.

"Raising yourself" is a tough challenge, but you can do it. So make the right choices now and give it all you've got.

Wishing you the best in your search for happiness and success in life,

—Sumant

I f you liked this book and would like to pass a copy on to someone else, please check with your local bookstore, online bookseller, or use a copy of this form:

Name _____ . _____

Address _____

City _____ State _____ Zip _____

Payment by: ☐ Check   ☐ Credit Card

Credit Card Number: _____

Expiration Date: _____

Check which: ☐ MasterCard   ☐ Visa

Raising Yourself ____ copies @ $11.95 each $ _____

California residents, please add applicable sales tax $ _____

Shipping: $3.95/first copy; $2.00 each additional copy* $ _____

Total enclosed, or charge my credit card (above) $ _____

For more than 5 copies, please contact the publisher for quantity rates. Send completed order form and your credit card information, check, or money order to:

Hillview Books
Order Department
P.O. Box 3473
Los Altos, CA 94024

or order via our Web Site at www.hillviewbooks.com

*International shipping is extra. Please contact us for the shipping rates to your location, if outside the United States.